OF A
ROMAN CATHOLIC

by

Paul Whitcomb

*"He that heareth you, heareth me;
and he that despiseth you, despiseth
me; and he that despiseth me,
despiseth him that sent me."*
—Luke 10:16

TAN BOOKS AND PUBLISHERS, INC.
Rockford, Illinois 61105

Nihil Obstat: Rev. Edmund J. Bradley
                  Censor Deputatus

Imprimatur: ✠ Timothy Manning
                  Auxiliary Bishop of Los Angeles
                  Vicar General
                  December 23, 1958

Formerly published by Loyola Book Co., Los Angeles, California.

340,000 copies distributed.

ISBN: 0-89555-281-7

Printed and bound in the United States of America.

TAN BOOKS AND PUBLISHERS, INC.
P.O. Box 424
Rockford, Illinois 61105

1985

*Dedicated to
the Unification of All Christians
within the Mystical Body
of Jesus Christ*

Paul Whitcomb

Gift better than Himself God doth
   not know,

Gift better than his God no man
   can see;

This gift doth here the giver given
   bestow

Gift to this gift let each receiver
   be:

God is my gift, Himself He freely
   gave me,

God's gift am I, and none but God
   shall have me.

> —St. Robert Southwell
>   *16th century English priest*
>   *martyred during*
>   *the Protestant Reformation*

INTRODUCTION

So that the title will not mislead anyone, it should be pointed out that this booklet is NOT a transcript of a Roman Catholic confessing his sins in the Sacrament of Penance. Nor is this booklet a *critique* on a particular church or religious faith. This "confession" is simply a graphic recounting of a rather extraordinary spiritual odyssey, a spiritual odyssey which had its finale in the Catholic Church. This is simply a testimonial of one man's faith, *an intimate glimpse of one man's soul.* Viewed in the broad sense one might call this a study of the Catholic *psyche,* for contained in this testimonial is the basic Catholic motivation, the reason why *all* Catholics are Catholics. To get the most out of the author's narrative, however, one really should view it in the narrow sense, that is, as an individual religious experience confided privately, person to person, for then one will more fully recognize the sincerity and good will that inspired it, and more fully appreciate the unreserved frankness of its presentation. But viewed either way this booklet is sure to provide a memorable reading experience.

vii

CONFESSION
OF A
ROMAN CATHOLIC

Yes, dear reader, I am a Catholic, or "Roman" Catholic, if you prefer. I recognize the Pope as the Vicar of Christ on earth, I worship God at that solemn rite called the Holy Sacrifice of the Mass, I venerate the Blessed Virgin Mary and I confess my sins to a priest.

I am one of those people who harbor the conviction that the Catholic Church is the one true Church of Jesus Christ.

And if you happen to be of another religious faith, particularly if you happen to be a Protestant, I have a pretty good idea what you are thinking. You are probably thinking: "Poor deluded fellow ... it is a pity that he has never been exposed to the light of Scripture, a pity that he does not enjoy the intellectual freedom enjoyed by other Christians ... for if he had the least familiarity with Sacred Scripture, the least freedom of intellectual inquiry, he would never subscribe to such a faith ... he would be a Protestant, or an Eastern Orthodox, or an unaffiliated Christian—anything but a Roman Catholic."

This is likely to be your opinion. In fact, if you did not regard me as something of a religious oddity I would be very surprised. You hear so many stories about the "strange goings on" in the Catholic Church, and so many of these stories purport to be "authoritative" reports on Catholic belief

1

and practice—what else can you think? If you did not attach some credence to these stories, or at least entertain some lively suspicions, you just would not be a "normal" non-Catholic.

Before you pass final judgment, however, there is something I feel you should know: I have a confession to make. I have something to tell you that will undoubtedly surprise you and strike you as being altogether incredible; but believe me, dear reader, it is the truth—every word of it.

All of the stories you have heard about the unscriptural and totalitarian character of the Catholic Church notwithstanding, it was my pursuit of Scriptural truth and my exercise of intellectual freedom that led me to become a Catholic.

I mean that! But for the fact that I *was* exposed to the light of Scripture, but for the fact that I *do* enjoy freedom of intellectual inquiry, *and but for the fact that I found all those accusations against the Catholic Church to be thoroughly untrue,* I would, in all probability, have this day the same opinion of Catholics that you have.

You see, I have not always been a Catholic. For the first 32 years of my life I was a Protestant. And what is more, I was a through and through Protestant. I was born of Protestant parents—an Episcopalian father and a Methodist mother. I was baptized a Protestant—Episcopal because my brother before me was baptized a Methodist. I was reared a Protestant—sent regularly to Episcopal, Methodist, Congregational, and Baptist Sunday schools, whichever was handiest to where we lived, and enlisted in various Protestant youth movements. My parents were staunch "liberal" Protestants: they believed that one church is as good as another—so long as it is Christian and Protestant.

As might be expected, when I reached manhood I married a Protestant—a devout Augustana-Synod Lutheran. Then began my stint, for the sake of domestic harmony, in the Lutheran faith. I say my "stint" in the Lutheran faith, because within a year's time my wife and I were obliged by economic considerations to move to another section of the country where, except for a sprinkling of Baptists and Pentecostals, all of the Protestants were Methodist. There I became active once again in the Methodist Church, my wife joining with me (I think that, with the possible exception of Missouri-Synod Lutherans and some Southern Baptists, all Protestants are liberals at heart), and there I decided to become, and in due course did become, a Methodist minister.

Yes, for 32 years, through childhood and well into adulthood, my environment was strictly a Protestant environment, my creed strictly a Protestant creed. If ever there were a "thoroughbred" Protestant, it was I.

And I say that without any misgivings. Why should I have misgivings? My association with Protestantism did me a great deal of good. It was as a Protestant that I learned of the reality and power and munificent goodness of God. It was as a Protestant that I learned of Jesus Christ, the only-begotten Son of God, come into the world to atone for the sins of man and lead man in the way of eternal salvation. *It was as a Protestant that I learned to acknowledge and revere the Bible as the holy Word of God.* And it was as a Protestant that I came to know many wonderful God-fearing people, people whose sincerity and genuine Christian charity were a great source of inspiration to me.

It would be deceitful and most ungrateful of me to deny that I benefited from my long association with Protestantism. In all Christian truthfulness I must admit that those were good days, so good I still feel a very pleasant nostalgia whenever they are recalled to memory.

However, be that as it may, I had to make a change. *In conscience I had to become a Catholic.*

Divine Providence just would not have it any other way. To be sure, I was an avid student of the Bible—I believed that the Bible is the sole

4

Christian rule of faith. But, as Divine Providence would have it, the more I studied the Bible, and the more I made it my rule of faith, the more I realized that my faith was not wholly what God had ordered. I discovered *voids* in my religious fabric, voids which had to be filled if I were to know real peace of soul. This feeling of spiritual insecurity led me inexorably to a study of comparative religion; and, again as Divine Providence would have it, the more I studied comparative religion the more I came to realize that the Catholic faith was the one faith that could fill the voids in my religious life, the one faith that could give me the real peace of soul I longed for.

"Poppycock! Pure figments of the imagination!" you will say. And again I say that may indeed be your honest opinion. But I also say, read on. For if you will read on and not draw hasty conclusions I think you will alter your opinion. Perhaps you will not sympathize with my explanation, but I am sure you will find that I am not relating something that happened solely in my imagination.

A really conscientious student of the Bible does not imagine what he reads there, and as I said before, after entering the Methodist ministry I was just that, a really conscientious student of the Bible. I practically lived in the Bible, for not only did I consider it expedient that I should be constantly

5

enlarging upon my knowledge of Scripture text, so that I could preach with more and more fluency, I also considered it expedient that I should be constantly enlarging upon my knowledge of Scripture exegesis (correct interpretation), so that I could preach with more and more authority. To be a proficient quoter of Scripture was not enough—I also wanted to be a proficient *explainer* of Scripture. Particularly, I wanted to be able to explain the indistinct passages of Scripture, the passages most Protestant ministers pass over on the grounds that they are "too ambiguous" for explanation; for it was my considered opinion that those passages contained some very significant truths, truths that *could* be brought to light and *should* be brought to light.

In short, I wanted to preach God's *whole* revealed truth, and I wanted to be able to verify that it was His whole revealed truth. I wanted to be a *fully qualified* minister of the Gospel.

Now you can call this presumption if you want to, but I honestly do believe this program of mine was God-inspired. For, as it happened, my study of Scripture exegesis had hardly begun when I made a very remarkable discovery, a discovery which had the effect of removing all apprehension from my mind. I discovered that whenever I came across an indistinct, seemingly ambiguous, passage of Scripture, one which allowed for

6

several interpretations, I could remove the ambiguity, find the one true interpretation, by searching out other passages directly bearing on the subject and correlating them.

For example, Christ repeatedly refers to God in the Bible as "my" Father and to Himself as the "son" of God. When those passages are isolated, three distinct and contradictory interpretations can be drawn from them: 1) Jesus was a mortal being, a son of God in the same sense that all Christians are sons of God; 2) Jesus was a supernatural being, a son of God in the sense that visible angels are sons (emissaries) of God; (3) Jesus was a divine Being, a son of God in the sense that He was of the very Essence of God. But when those passages are not isolated, when they are correlated with Jesus' other statements bearing on His identity—e.g., *John* 1:18, 8:19, 10:38, 12:45 and 14:8-12—the one true interpretation, namely the third one, emerges clear as crystal. Hence the doctrine of the Holy Trinity, professed by the overwhelming majority of Christians, which defines God as being numerically and individually one in essence but existing in three Persons—God the Father, God the Son, and God the Holy Spirit.

This method of ascertaining the true intended meaning of indistinct Scripture passages— employed by all the leading authorities on Scripture exegesis, I later found out—brought a great deal of consolation to me because it established the scriptural validity of some tenets of faith I had previously taken for granted simply because they were traditional Protestant tenets. *But it also brought some surprising revelations, revelations I had not bargained for, revelations which challenged the scriptural validity of some of my beliefs.* In this I was not consoled but rather very disturbed.

The first of these surprising revelations had to do with the intrinsic structure of Christ's true church. In the most literal and absolute sense Christ's true church is a *body,* I learned. Further, this body is not a group body, like a body of people, but is an organic and spiritual entity, like the body of a single person. Further, this body, the true Christian Church, is not strictly a human body but is akin to being a divine body—*this is by virtue of the fact that it is the Mystical Body of Christ Himself.* Actually, albeit mystically, Christ's true faithful constitute the members of His church body, while He reigns in Heaven as the Head of His church body.

And where does the Bible say such a thing? This significant truism is expressed in a great number of Bible passages, but it is most apparent in the following:

"And he is the head of the body, the church."

8

(Col. 1:18). *"But now there are many members indeed, yet one body. . . . Now you are the body of Christ, and members of member."* (1 Cor. 12:20-27). *"Because we are members of his body, of his flesh, and of his bones."* (Eph. 5:30). *"For as in one body we have many members, but all the members have not the same office: So we being many, are one body in Christ, and every one members one of another."* (Rom. 12:4-5). *"Know you not that your bodies are the members of Christ?"* (1 Cor. 6:15).

Because the body of Christ is one body, His Church must perforce be one body also:

"There shall be one fold and one shepherd." (John 10:16). *"Careful to keep the unity of the Spirit in the bond of peace. One body and one Spirit; as you are called in one hope of your calling. One Lord, one faith, one baptism. One God and Father of all, who is above all, and through all, and in us all."* (Eph. 4:3-6). *"Now I beseech you, brethren, to mark them who make dissensions and offenses contrary to the doctrine which you have learned, and avoid them."* (Rom. 16:17).

Because a special supernatural grace was needed to cement *permanently* the unity of His

Church, Christ provided that special supernatural grace—*He had His Church sanctified in truth:*

> *"These things Jesus spoke, and lifting up his eyes to heaven, he said . . . Holy Father, keep them in thy name whom thou hast given me; that they may be one, as we also are. . . . Sanctify them in truth. Thy word is truth. . . . That they all may be one, as thou, Father, in me, and I in thee; that they also may be one in us. . . . I in them, and thou in me; that they may be made perfect in one."* (John 17:1-23).

In the face of such evidence how could I entertain any doubt? There it was plain as could be in Sacred Scripture, the Word of God, that Christ's true faithful constitute a single unified body—unified in every respect: in organization, in belief, and in worship. That was the way Christ's Mystical Body on earth was originally constituted, and in order for it to live on as His Mystical Body on earth that is the way it had to stay constituted.

It would have been foolhardy in the extreme for me to entertain doubts concerning the invincible oneness of Christ's Church; for not only was it self-evident in Sacred Scripture, it was self-evident in all of the writings of the primitive Church Fathers. Wrote the great St. Cyprian in the third century: "God is one and Christ is one, and one is

10

His Church, and the faith is one, and one His people welded together by the glue of concord into a solid unity of body. Unity cannot be rent asunder, nor can the one body of the Church, through the division of its structure, be divided into separate pieces." (St. Cyprian, *On the Unity of the Church,* chap. 23).

Likewise Tertullian in the third century: "We are a society with a single religious feeling, a single unity of discipline, a single bond of hope." (*Apology,* 39, 1).

Likewise St. Hilary in the fourth century: "In the Scriptures our people are shown to be made one; so that just as many grains collected into one and ground and mingled together, make one loaf, so in Christ, who is the heavenly Bread, we know that there is one body, in which our whole company is joined and united." (*Treatise* 62, 13).

Now I ask you, is it any wonder that my conscience was disturbed by this revelation? Behold, I was not a member of a Christian unity or body. As a Protestant I was part of a Christian "co-operative," an "interdenominational association" made up of over 300 Christian bodies, each one different in name, in belief, in government, and, to a lesser extent, in form of worship. True, they all professed Christ as Lord and Saviour, and they all professed to preach His Gospel—they all proclaimed that their primary objective was the salvation of souls. In that respect there was indeed a common identity, or sameness. But the fact still remained: They refused to meet on the same premises to profess their faith in Christ as Lord and Saviour, they disagreed as to what constitutes Christ's whole and true Gospel, and they were very much at odds concerning what qualifies a person for eternal salvation.

For example, one Protestant body held the independent view that altar and liturgy have no place in Christian worship. Another held the independent view that the sacraments should be withheld from infants and small children. Another held the independent view that man becomes impervious to sin and assured of salvation once he accepts Christ as his personal Saviour. Another held the independent view that membership in Christ's Church is restricted to a select few, and when one of the select few falls away from God's grace no amount of repentance can restore him. Another held the independent view that Saturday, not Sunday, is the Lord's Day. Another held the independent view that the powers of church administration reside not with the clergy but with the laity of the local congregation.

Yes, here within this interdenominational framework was fellowship—here was a genuine, concerted love and longing for Christ and His promise of salvation. That much had to be conceded. *But here also was division, division in the most explicit and flagrant sense of the word.* Here, unquestionably, was a concept of Christ's mystical Body on earth which could not possibly be consonant with the one spirit, one faith, one shepherd concept described in the Bible.

This realization distressed me more than I can say. Like His glorified body in Heaven, Christ's Mystical Body on earth never was and never will be a disjointed body, my conscience kept repeating—and I did so want to be joined to His true Mystical Body, that I might share in its bountiful graces, that I might be, as St. Paul said, a member of His body, of His flesh, and of His bones. (*Eph.* 5:30). The pleasantness of my Protestant association notwithstanding, I did so want to be ONE with Christ, my Salvation.

One passage of Scripture suddenly became very meaningful. Over and over I pondered these words: "Seek, and you shall find: knock, and it shall be opened to you." (*Matt.* 7:7). And at length I realized what I must do in order to placate my conscience. Just worrying over the situation would gain me nothing. If I were ever to find the unity which Christ said would distinguish His true faithful, I would have to *search* for it.

So down to the big public library I went—and I

commenced to search. I searched through every history of Christian church development I could find. I searched through the sectarian histories and the non-sectarian histories, the big encyclopedias and the little encyclopedias. I took special pains to be as comprehensive and as objective in my search as possible. Indeed, I took the same pains with these volumes as I did with the Holy Bible; for here again it was my own conscience I was serving; I would have been fooling no one but myself if I shirked any evidence or displayed even the slightest bias.

Then finally, after several weeks of intense searching and comparing, I found the blessed unity I was looking for. And I found it where I least expected to find it—*in the Roman Catholic Church.*

That was not easy to accept, believe me. I hated to think that the church I had been most opposed to was the church most united in Christ. But I had to be honest with myself. The spectacle of 825 million Catholics, three-fifths of all professed Christians, perfectly, indomitably united in belief, in organization, and in worship—the historical fact that Catholics, consistently the largest body of Christians in the world, have *always* been thus perfectly united—was evidence I could not ignore. Perhaps I was prejudiced, but I certainly was not blind.

Here was the unity of Bible prophecy—there was no doubt in my mind about that. It had to be! Nowhere else on the Christian scene was there a unity nearly so compact, nearly so long-lived. *Nowhere else on the Christian scene was there a unity so obviously permanent.*

However, finding the unity of Bible prophecy did not entirely settle the matter. Just as great as the problem of finding it, I found, was the problem of embracing it. What about the other aspects of Catholicism, I asked myself. What about Catholic doctrine, Catholic dogmatism, *Catholic authoritarianism.* Could I, in justice to my conscience, set aside my suspicions concerning those aspects of Catholicism merely for the sake of the unity of Catholicism?

Those questions posed quite a problem. But I solved that problem all right. After considerable soul searching I concluded that unity was indeed a precious and most important Christian commodity, but right doctrine and right authority were also precious, also important, perhaps even more so. Therefore, I should play it safe: I should preserve the status quo of my religious affiliation, at least for the time being, and get back to my Bible studies. The prospect of having to interrupt my Bible studies did not set too well with me anyway.

That was a wise decision, you will say. But I

say that it was a *Providential* decision, a *God-inspired* decision. For lo, I had no sooner returned to my beloved Scripture studies when along came another revelation, a revelation even more significant than the first one. Yes, and it was every bit as disturbing.

Clear as day I saw in Sacred Scripture that Christ's true church is not the "learning" church I had always believed it to be, but is manifestly a TEACHING church. Moreover, it was quite evident that Christ's true church is an INFALLIBLE teacher, never liable to teach false doctrine.

The key that opened the door of my conscience to this truth was Christ's directive to His Apostles shortly before His Ascension into Heaven:

"All power is given to me in heaven and in earth. Going therefore, teach ye all nations; baptizing them in the name of the Father, and of the Son, and of the Holy Ghost. Teaching them to observe all things whatsoever I have commanded you: and behold I am with you all days, even to the consummation of the world." (Matt. 28:18-20).

The teaching mission of His Church could not have been more clearly pronounced if Christ had devoted a great long sermon to it. Those two sentences were direct and peremptory enough to rule out any possibility of misinterpretation.

Then there was His statement to the Apostles on another occasion, telling them: "As the Father hath sent me, I also send you." (*John* 20:21). Here again is a clear, unmistakable reference to the teaching mission of His Church; for here He is telling the Apostles that they had fallen heir to His own teaching mission. *His Church was to be no less of a teacher than He was.*

Further, it was quite obvious that Christ did not give this teaching authority to all and sundry, that is, to the *whole* Church, but only to His duly appointed Apostles, those who were to be the *administrative body* of the Church. Had He meant that this teaching authority was to be exercised by all of the faithful He would have addressed His words to all of the faithful, or He would have instructed the Apostles to so advise all of the faithful—neither of which He did. The Bible is quite clear on that score. Some have been placed in the Church as teachers, not all, wrote the Apostle Paul. (*1 Cor.* 12:28-29).

Now where did I get the idea that the teaching authority of Christ's Church cannot err when it defines the essentials of Christian doctrine? Where did I get the idea that this teaching authority can no more err today than it could in the beginning when it was held by the Apostles? I got the idea from Christ Himself—*by correlating His statements concerning the teaching authority of His Church with His statements concerning the divine protection pledged to that teaching authority.* Said Christ to the Apostles:

> *"These things have I spoken to you, abiding with you. But the Paraclete, the Holy Ghost, whom the Father will send in my name, he will teach you all things, and bring all things to your mind, whatsoever I shall have said to you. . . . when the Paraclete cometh, whom I will send you from the Father, the Spirit of truth, who proceedeth from the Father, he shall give testimony of me. And you shall give testimony, because you are with me from the beginning."* (John 14:25-26; 15:26-27).

In other words, the teaching authority of Christ's Church would not, could not, teach error, because fallible human beings would not be doing the actual teaching. The infallible Holy Spirit of God, *the infallible Christ,* would be doing the actual teaching, speaking *through* the human teaching authority of the Church. Our Blessed Lord made this quite clear when He said to His disciples: *"He that heareth you, heareth me; and he that despiseth you, despiseth me; and he that despiseth me, despiseth him that sent me."* (Luke 10:16).

Confirming that the teaching authority of the Church is the perennial and infallible voice of Christian truth, the Apostle Paul wrote:

"These things I write to thee... that thou mayest know how thou oughtest to behave thyself in the house of God, which is the church of the living God, the pillar and ground of the truth." (1 Tim. 3:14-15).

And then there was the testimony of the primitive Christian Fathers. A cursory study of their writings disclosed that they also believed that Christ's Church is incapable of teaching error. Wrote the great St. Irenaeus in the second century: "For where the Church is, there is the Spirit of God; and where the Spirit of God is, there is the Church in every form of grace, for the Spirit of God is Truth." (*Against the Heresies,* 3, 24, 1).

And finally there was the testimony of my own faith. After pondering the matter, my own latent Christian faith insisted that Christ would not have admonished sinners to "hear the Church" unless He was sure they would be hearing the truth; nor would He have assured the Church that her pronouncements would be "bound in heaven" unless He was sure that her pronouncements contained no error. (*Matt.* 18:17-18). *Careful analysis of Christ's teachings revealed that faith in the*

19

doctrinal infallibility of His Church is synonymous with faith in Him.

Yes, Christ's Church just had to be both a teaching church and an *infallible* teaching church. The evidence of Sacred Scripture was just too overwhelming to permit any other conclusion.

Now let me explain why I was disturbed by this revelation. I was disturbed, dear reader, because I obviously was not a member of a divinely authorized teaching church, much less an infallible teaching church. The church I was a member of repudiated the whole idea of a divinely authorized teaching church. It maintained that no man or council on earth possesses the God-given authority to pronounce, as binding on the Christian conscience, what is and is not true Christian doctrine.

Here I was a "minister of the Gospel," yet I could not mount the pulpit and say: "Learn of me, for I teach with the authority of the Lord. Learn of me, for he who hears me hears Him." Nor could my bishop make such a declaration. Nor could the highest official in the church make such a declaration. Any minister or church official who dared make such a declaration would have been liable to the charge of heresy—he would have been accused of "Popery," which was the same thing as heresy.

20

It was perfectly all right to mount the pulpit and say, "Learn of me." In fact, we were duty bound to teach when we preached. But to say that we had direct authority from God to teach, to imply that our teaching bore the stamp of divine infallibility—that definitely was out. That would have been a serious breach of one of the most basic and fundamental tenets of Protestantism: the tenet that the Bible is the only divinely authorized dispenser and guarantor of Christian truth.

This idea that the Bible is the supreme and final arbiter of Christian truth had to dominate the theme of every sermon. We ministers had to make it quite clear that while it was good and edifying to hear the voice of the church, in the final analysis it was direct to the Bible, to the "constitution" of the church, that the Christian must needs go for the binding convictions of his faith. It had to be emphasized that the primary mission of the church was not so much to teach Christ's saving faith as it was to lead people to the Bible so that the Bible could teach them Christ's saving faith.

This despite the fact that for the first four hundred years of Christianity there was no published Christian Bible; this despite the fact that for the next one thousand years, until the invention of the printing press, there were scant few Bibles; this despite the fact that only the literate have ac-

21

cess to the Bible; this despite the fact that those who have made the Bible their sole rule of faith have come up with literally hundreds of conflicting rules of faith—this despite the fact that the Bible itself states that many who interpret it privately will interpret it wrongly, to their own destruction: ". . . in which [St. Paul's epistles] are certain things hard to be understood, which the unlearned and unstable wrest, as they do also the other scriptures, to their own destruction." (2 Peter 3:16).

The more I thought of it the more I thanked God for His wonderful revelation.

However, do not misunderstand me. I was not beginning to doubt the whole truth of the Bible, nor was I doubting the value of the Bible where Christian learning is concerned. These things I shall never doubt. I was simply facing up to the fact that the Bible, venerable book of truth that it is, is not the teacher of its own truth. The obvious was forcing itself upon me: Instead of being a teacher of God's truth, the Bible is a *catalog* of the truths God wants taught, and taught so that all Christian generations, including the blind and illiterate of those generations, can hear and understand.

Hence the Church.

Quite obviously, a living church possessed of an audible voice was needed to carry the great tidings of Salvation to all generations; therefore God in the Person of Jesus Christ founded such a church, and He said to it: "Go ye into the whole world, and preach the gospel to every creature." (*Mark* 16:15). Note that He said *preach* His Gospel to every creature, not distribute His Gospel to every creature in the form of a book. He ordered His Church to *speak* to the world because through His Church *He* would be speaking to the world. (*Luke* 10:16). How anything so obvious could have escaped me before, I do not know, unless my training had erected a mental block. It certainly is as plain as can be in Sacred Scripture.

Now my earnest desire was to seek out this church that could teach with the voice and authority of the Lord. I wanted this singularly blessed church to teach me. I wanted the wonderful assurance of Christ's own personal guarantee that my Christian faith was the true Christian faith prescribed by Him for the salvation of my soul.

So the months that followed found me once again engrossed in a great assortment of books on comparative Christian religion. Once again the library and all of the sectarian book stores in the vicinity became my favorite spare time haunts.

And once again my search ended where I least expected it to.

23

That is right, dear reader, the church I was looking for turned out to be none other than the same Catholic Church. How could I conscientiously say that it was not? My study of the doctrines and practices of the various Christian churches revealed most clearly that only one, the Catholic Church, exercises the same kind of teaching authority that was exercised by the church of the Apostles and primitive Church Fathers. Only the Catholic Church functions for her members as an unerring interpreter of God's revealed truth. Only the Catholic Church dares proclaim to the world that when she teaches the truths of Christian doctrine, it is Jesus Christ, who can neither deceive nor be deceived, teaching through her.

Only the Catholic Church was NAMED by the primitive Christian Fathers as the church appointed by Jesus Christ to carry on His sacred teaching ministry. Wrote St. Irenaeus in the second century: "The Catholic Church, having received the apostolic teaching and faith, though spread over the whole world, guards it sedulously, as though dwelling in one house; and these truths she uniformly teaches, as having but one soul and one heart; these truths she proclaims, teaches, and hands down as though she had but one mouth." (*Adv. Haer.*, 1, x, 2).

Wrote St. Eusebius of Caesarea in the fourth

century: "But the brightness of the Catholic Church proceeded to increase in greatness, for it ever held to the same points in the same way, and radiated forth to all the race of Greeks and barbarians the reverent, sincere, and free nature, and the sobriety and purity of the divine teaching as to conduct and thought." (*Ecclesiastical History,* 4, 7, 13).

Wrote St. Augustine in the fifth century: "The Catholic Church is the work of Divine Providence, achieved through the prophecies of the prophets, through the Incarnation and the teaching of Christ, through the journeys of the Apostles, through the suffering, the crosses, the blood and death of the martyrs, through the admirable lives of the saints, and in all these, at opportune times, through miracles worthy of such great deeds and virtues. When, then, we see so much help on God's part, so much progress and so much fruit, shall we hesitate to bury ourselves in the bosom of that Church? For starting from the apostolic chair down through successions of bishops, even unto the open confession of all mankind, it has possessed the crown of teaching authority." (*De Utilitate Credendi*).

Confirming that the primitive Catholic Church and the Roman Catholic Church were one and the same church, St. Ignatius of Antioch, a disciple of the Apostle John, wrote in the second century:

"Ignatius, also called Theophorus, to the Church that has found mercy in the transcendent Majesty of the Most High Father and of Jesus Christ, His only Son; the church by the will of Him who willed all things, beloved and illuminated through the faith and love of Jesus Christ our God; presiding in the chief place of the Roman territory . . . presiding in love, maintaining the law of Christ, and bearer of the Father's name: her do I therefore salute in the name of Jesus Christ." (Introduction—*To the Church of Rome*).

How significant and thought-provoking those statements of the primitive Christian Fathers are. How significant that every time they mentioned the teaching church of Jesus Christ it was the Catholic Church, never one of the Coptic churches, or one of the Orthodox churches, or one of the Protestant churches. And who should know better than they which Christian church is the true teaching church of Jesus Christ, the teaching church described in the holy Bible?

I know, about now you are probably thinking: "If the Catholic Church is the teaching church described in Bible prophecy, why does she suppress the Bible? Why does she bypass the Bible by drawing upon tradition for some of her articles of faith? *Why does she indulge in such unscriptural practices as praying to Christ's mother Mary?*"

My reply to that, dear friend, is this: Go to the Catholic Church as I went to the Catholic Church; conduct an on-the-spot investigation of Catholic teaching and practice as I did; and you will find out, as I found out, that all those stories about the Catholic Church suppressing and bypassing the Bible are as false as false can be. And you will find out that there is absolutely nothing unscriptural about praying to Christ's Blessed Mother.

I realize that this is a lot to ask. Like me you have probably been taught to distrust and stay strictly away from everything labeled Roman Catholic. But, believe me, you *must* go to the Catholic Church if you want complete and accurate knowledge of her teachings and practices.

You certainly would not go to the Swiss Information Bureau for authoritative information on the winter resorts of Norway, or to General Motors for authoritative information on the performance of Ford automobiles, or to a staunch Democrat for authoritative information on the achievements and aspirations of the Republican Party. Nor would you seek authoritative information about the former from the latter. Why? Because it is just not fair to obtain information about something, or someone, from a rival. It is not fair to yourself, and it certainly is not fair to your subject. Rival information is always prejudiced information, and therefore is seldom entirely free of serious omissions and gross exaggerations.

Why, then, trust another church to give you completely reliable information about the teachings and practices of the Catholic Church?

That was the simple rule of logic and fairness I adopted, and I must say that it rewarded me beyond measure. Instead of finding the Bible suppressed in the Catholic Church, I found it very much in evidence and very highly honored. In fact, I had never before visited a church where the Bible was so much in evidence, so highly honored. I noticed that during Mass an enormous and exceedingly beautiful book filled with Scripture, called the *Missal,* rests on the altar and occupies much of the priest's attention as he proceeds through the Mass liturgy. I noticed that during Low Mass the priest raises this great book of Scripture to his lips and reverently kisses it, and during High Mass he solemnly incenses it, signifying the Church's loving devotion to God's revealed truth. And I noticed that the priest celebrant of the Mass, or a priest assistant, never preaches the Mass sermon without first taking a New Testament and reading some Epistle and Gospel verses to the congregation, and never without first offering up this prayer with the congregation: "The Lord be in my heart and on my lips, that I may worthily and in a becoming manner proclaim His holy Gospel." *I noticed that throughout the whole course of the Mass, which is the center and heart of all Catholic worship, there was a most profound reverence shown to Sacred Scripture by all present.* At the reading of the Gospel, for example, everyone stands in reverence of the Word.

And that is not all. I found that this reverence has been manifest in the worship of the Catholic Church since the fourth century when the Christian canon of Sacred Scripture was first determined—and determined, incidentally, by this same Catholic Church. *Catholic devotion to the Bible is as old as the Bible itself.*

Are Catholics encouraged to read and meditate upon the Scriptures privately in their own homes? Indeed they are. Contrary to what many Protestants think—contrary to what I myself had long believed—Catholics are constantly being told, in sermons, in letters from their Bishop, and in Papal encyclicals, the spiritual good that will come from keeping a Bible in the home and daily meditating on its content. Wrote Pope Pius XII in the Encyclical Letter, *On the Promotion of Biblical Studies:* "For the Sacred Books were not given by God to men to satisfy their curiosity or to provide them with material for study and research, but, as the Apostle observes, in order that these Divine Oracles might 'instruct us to

29

salvation, by the faith which is in Christ Jesus,' and 'that the man of God may be perfect, furnished to every good work.'" Bishops should help "excite and foster among Catholics a greater knowledge of and love for the Sacred Books. Let them favor, therefore, and lend help to those pious associations whose aim it is to spread copies of the Sacred Letters, especially of the Gospels, among the faithful, and to procure by every means that in Christian families the same be read daily with piety and devotion. . . . for, as St. Jerome, the Doctor of Stridon, says: 'To ignore the Scripture is to ignore Christ.'"

No, there definitely is no suppression of the Bible in the Catholic Church. All who believe otherwise have been grossly misinformed.

Concerning the allegation that the Catholic Church "bypasses" the Bible when she bases some of her articles of faith on tradition, I merely had to focus my attention on a few passages of the Bible itself to be convinced that this allegation is totally without foundation in fact. Strange I had not noticed this before, but the Bible does actually state that some of Christ's teachings were committed to tradition; that is to say, they were handed down by word of mouth rather than by letter. Further, the Bible actually states that these teachings were no less important for having been committed to tradition. Here are the Bible passages to which I was referred:

> *"Therefore, brethren, stand fast; and hold the traditions which you have learned, whether by word or by our epistle."* (2 Thess. 2:14). *"And we charge you, brethren, in the name of our Lord Jesus Christ, that you withdraw yourselves from every brother walking disorderly, and not according to the tradition which they have received of us."* (2 Thess. 3:6).

There is no questioning the meaning of those sentences. Here the Apostle Paul specifically states that there is not one but *two* criteria of Christian truth: that which was left to the Church via the Bible, via the *written* word, and that which was left to the Church via tradition, via the *unwritten* word—both of which, he says, are of equal importance to the faith of Christians.

And why was it necessary to bequeath some tenets of Christ's saving faith to the Church via the unwritten word, by word of mouth rather than by letter? Again the Bible furnishes the answer:

> *"This is that disciple who giveth testimony of these things, and hath written these things; and we know that his testimony is true. But there are also many other things which Jesus did; which, if they were written every one, the*

world itself, I think, would not be able to contain the books that should be written." (John 21:24-25).

So we have the Bible's own word for it that there were some things which Jesus said and did, some things which the Apostles taught, that were not written down, that did not find their way into the Bible—not because they were relatively unimportant *but because writing it all down with the means and time available would have been humanly impossible.* Had the Apostles and their disciples attempted to record all of Our Lord's doings and teachings they would have had no time left for preaching and baptizing and organizing the Church in the far-flung mission fields, which was what Christ had ordered them to do.

Now the question arises: What made me so sure that the tradition which forms the basis of part of Catholic doctrine is the tradition, the unrecorded teachings of Christ, mentioned in the Bible? A little objective research, plus a little objective Christian reasoning, made me sure. First of all there was the testimony of the primitive Christian Fathers. Wrote St. Athanasius in the fourth century: "But it will hardly be out of place to investigate likewise the ancient traditions, and the doctrines and faith of the Catholic Church, which the Lord communicated, the Apostles proclaimed, and the Fathers preserved; for on this has the

Church been founded." Wrote St. Augustine in the fifth century: "These traditions of the Christian name, therefore, so numerous, so powerful, and most dear, justly keep a believing man in the Catholic Church."

Then I went back over the mainstream of Christian belief and practice since Christianity began, and discovered, much to my surprise, that all the other ancient and semi-ancient Christian churches—Coptic, Greek Orthodox and Russian Orthodox—have consistently held to the same tradition-based doctrines that the Catholic Church holds to, *proving that acceptance of them was universal prior to the advent of Protestantism in 1517.*

Also it occurred to me that if the tradition which forms the basis of part of Catholic doctrine is not the tradition mentioned in the Bible, what has become of it? Could it be that some of Christ's teachings have become extinct? To this I had to answer in the conscience of my faith that after suffering ignominy on the Cross to plant His truth in the world, Christ would not permit any part of it to become extinct. "Heaven and earth shall pass away, but my word shall not pass away," He said. (*Mark* 13:31).

So there it was, all the evidence I needed to be thoroughly convinced that Catholic tradition is

Bible tradition. In basing part of her doctrine on tradition the Catholic Church quite obviously is not bypassing the Bible, but *complying* with the Bible.

Manifestly clear to me now was the justification for such Catholic practices as praying to Heaven for the intercession of Mary and the saints. *For these practices are the traditions referred to in the Bible.* They have to be the traditions referred to in the Bible, otherwise why were they so precious to the primitive Christians?

To give you an idea how precious these traditions were to the primitive Christians I refer you to St. Ephraem's *Prayer to the most holy Mother of God,* composed by that illustrious deacon in the fourth century: "O Virgin Lady, immaculate Mother of God, my lady most glorious, most gracious, much purer than the sun's splendor, budding staff of Aaron, you appeared as a true staff, and the flower is your Son our true Christ, my God and Maker. You bore God and the Word according to the flesh, preserving your virginity before childbirth, a virgin after childbirth, and we have been reconciled with Christ, God your Son."

Then there is this prayer, composed by St. Germanus of Constantinople in the seventh century: "O Lady, all-chaste, all-good, rich in mercy, comfort of Christians, tender consoler of the afflicted, the ever-open refuge of sinners, do not leave us destitute of thy assistance. Shelter us under the wings of thy goodness. By thy intercession watch over us."

Indeed, I could go on and on, quoting Bible passage after Bible passage, Church Father after Church Father, until several volumes were filled, displaying the evidence which convinced me that *Catholic tradition is Bible tradition, and therefore part and parcel of the Christian deposit of faith.*

But, alas, as convincing as this great mass of evidence was, I still did not have the strength of will to hand myself over to the Catholic Church. Force of habit is a mighty force, I found, quite capable of resisting some of the strongest mental persuasions. It plays tricks on the mind, it anesthetizes the mind, it creates the illusion in the mind that custom, somehow, is a profound truth in itself, a truth which, for some mysterious reason, transcends all other truths.

Somehow I managed to convince myself that I was a Protestant by the irrevocable force of heredity, like my skin was white by the irrevocable force of heredity; therefore I should not change the complexion of things like this because it was God's doing. In other words, I was a Protestant "by nature," therefore the "natural" thing for me to do was remain a Protestant. Certainly

God would make allowances on the Judgment Day for people who just naturally were not Catholics, I told myself, providing, of course, they believed in Him with their whole heart and soul and repented of their sins, which I did.

However, force of habit and all the excuses I conjured up were no match for the grace of God. It was not long before my eyes were opened to yet another Bible revelation, one so rife with eternal consequences that there could be no resistance, no excuses. Had I remained out of the Catholic Church after this truth was made known to me I would have had to abandon my conscience altogether—I would have had to lift my eyes to Heaven and say, "Not Thy will, Lord, but *mine* be done."

Speaking right out of my Bible, Christ my Lord said to me:

"I am the bread of life. Your fathers did eat manna in the desert, and are dead. This is the bread which cometh down from heaven; that if any man eat of it, he may not die. I am the living bread which came down from heaven. If any man eat of this bread, he shall live for ever; and the bread that I will give, is my flesh, for the life of the world." (John 6:48-52).

I contemplated those words long and hard, for while I had read them many times before and found them beautiful and stirring, I now saw in them something extremely personal and challenging, something that demanded clarification. You see, I had been led to believe that in this text Christ was speaking figuratively, that is, the bread He promised to give for the life of the world was not to be construed as His actual self, but bread *symbolic,* or *representative,* of His self. But somehow the more I contemplated His words the more I suspected that there was something drastically wrong with this interpretation. How, I asked myself, can symbolic bread be called "living" bread? How can symbolic bread vivify and impart divine life to the soul? *How can dead vegetable substance be representative of the living Son of God?*

Faced with these perplexing questions, I sought for the answers elsewhere in Sacred Scripture—I resorted to "interpretation by correlation," the method of interpretation that had served me so well before. And again this method did not fail me. A close analysis of all the pertinent Bible texts revealed that the Jews did not understand Christ to mean symbolical bread. *They understood Him to mean bread that consisted of His true and living flesh.* "How can this man give us his flesh to eat?" they argued. (*John* 6:53). Christ was speaking not in the figurative sense but in the literal sense, those Jews surmised; and they must have surmised correctly because Christ made no attempt to change their thinking; instead, He repeated Himself, laying even greater stress on the literal sense of His words:

"Amen, amen I say unto you: Except you eat the flesh of the Son of man, and drink his blood, you shall not have life in you. He that eateth my flesh, and drinketh my blood, hath everlasting life: and I will raise him up in the last day. For my flesh is meat indeed: and my blood is drink indeed." (John 6:54-56).

No, He did not retract even when many of His disciples, likewise scandalized at the literal implication of His words, deserted Him. (*John* 6:67). He even told the Apostles that they, too, could desert Him before He would subtract one iota from the literal import of His words. (*John* 6:68).

Christ must have meant exactly what He said. In truth He must have intended to nourish mankind with the divine soul-saving food of His own Flesh and Blood, otherwise He would not have been so adamant, so unswervingly specific.

But how? How could the faithful actually partake of His true and living Flesh and Blood? That was what the Jews wanted to know and that was

38

what I wanted to know. Only there was this difference between the Jews and myself: Like the Apostles, I had faith that somehow it could be done; like the Apostles, I believed that with Christ, with Divinity, all things are possible; like the Apostles, I exercised patience and was rewarded for my patience. Searching the Scriptures further I learned exactly how Christ intended to give His Flesh and Blood for the faithful to eat and drink—*I found the full explanation contained in the account of the Last Supper:*

"And whilst they were at supper, Jesus took bread, and blessed, and broke: and gave to his disciples, and said: Take ye, and eat. THIS IS MY BODY. And taking the chalice, he gave thanks, and gave to them, saying: Drink ye all of this. FOR THIS IS MY BLOOD." (cf. Matt. 26:26-28; Mark 14:22-24; Luke 22:19-20).

The bread and wine of Holy Communion, that was it! The bread and wine of Holy Communion were not mere symbols, or representations, of Christ's Body, as I had been led to believe, but were in very truth bread and wine miraculously transformed by the power of God into Christ's true and living Flesh and Blood, only the *appearance* of bread and wine remaining. Not only did I have Christ's promise at Capharnaum and the fulfillment of Christ's promise at the Last Supper to convince me of this, I had the testimony of the Apostles, preached to the whole infant Christian community. In the most unequivocal language the Apostles affirmed that the bread and wine duly consecrated on the altar did in fact become the *actual Substance* of the Saviour. Declared the Apostle Paul:

> *"The chalice of benediction which we bless, is it not the communion of the blood of Christ? And the bread which we break, is it not the partaking of the body of the Lord?"* (1 Cor. 10:16). *"But let a man prove himself: and so let him eat of that bread, and drink of the chalice. For he that eateth and drinketh unworthily, eateth and drinketh judgment to himself, not discerning the body of the Lord."* (1 Cor. 11:28-29).

What further proof did I need? None at all, for the Bible was my criterion of Christian truth and the Bible could not have been more explicit. Yet, lest there be some lingering suspicions, I sought out the belief of the primitive Christian Fathers. If anyone were qualified to pass judgment on the correctness of my conclusion it was they, for they were the disciples, the immediate successors, of the Apostles—their interpretation of Sacred Scripture was obtained firsthand from the very authors of Sacred Scripture.

40

It turned out that the primitive Christian Fathers had a great deal to say on the subject, and it turned out that all of them were in perfect agreement. Those illustrious leaders of the infant Christian Church called the bread and wine consecrated on the altar the "Eucharist," and they unanimously maintained that by virtue of the consecration it was no longer common food-stuff but had become, by the Omnipotent Power of God, the true Flesh and Blood of the Saviour.

Wrote St. Ignatius of Antioch, disciple of the Apostle John, concerning the heretics of his day: "They have abstained from the Eucharist and prayer, because they do not confess that the Eucharist is the flesh of Our Saviour Jesus Christ."

Wrote St. Justin Martyr, another Church Father of the second century: "This food is known among us as the Eucharist ... We do not receive these things as common bread and common drink; but as Jesus Christ our Saviour, being made flesh by the Word of God."

Wrote St. Cyril of Jerusalem, venerable Church Father of the fourth century: "Since then He has declared and said of the bread, 'This is my body,' who after that will venture to doubt? And seeing that He has affirmed and said, 'This is my blood,' who will raise a question and say it is not His blood?"

Now I knew with absolute certainty that I was right. Not only did the Church Fathers confirm the correctness of my interpretation, they did so most emphatically. And so did all of the great Christian apologists of succeeding centuries. Indeed, I found that it was not until comparatively recent times, until modernism began infecting Christianity with its fondness for reckless theorizing, that any professed Christian held a contrary view.

What a predicament! There in the Bible was Christ my Lord telling me that I needed to eat of His Flesh and drink of His Blood in order to have eternal happiness with Him in Heaven; there in the Bible was the Apostle Paul telling me that I should prove my faith by discerning the Body and Blood of Christ in the consecrated bread and wine of the altar; there in history were the Church Fathers condemning as heretics all Christians who do not associate themselves with the Real Presence; and there I was without this divine soul-saving food, without this discernible Body and Blood of Christ on the altar, without this blessed association with the Real Presence.

There I was with my eternal salvation in obvious jeopardy.

42

It was a desperate situation, one that called for immediate and positive action. And act I did, following the same positive course of action I am sure you would have followed, dear friend in Christ, under identical circumstances: I went calling on churches, I went in search of that particular church which could give me the true and living Christ in Holy Communion, not common everyday bread and wine such as I could find down at the corner market place.

First I called on the other Protestant churches, hoping upon hope that one of them would have the true Eucharistic Christ. But no success. Wherever I called, the answer was negative. Invariably the consecrated bread and wine of Holy Communion were only "symbols" of Christ's Flesh and Blood, or were "abodes of His Spirit," or were "temples of His Sacramental Presence," or were "vehicles of His *hidden* Flesh and Blood," or were "bread and wine mysteriously *merged* with His Flesh and Blood." *Invariably the physical substance of bread and wine substituted for the physical Reality of Jesus Christ.*

Some ministers did indeed call their communion bread and wine the real Body and Blood of Christ, but invariably, when I pinned them down, asking if by "real" they meant *corporeal,* they said no. Invariably, when I asked if one receives a new influx of divine grace at their Holy Communion service, the answer was: "No, we believe that Holy Communion is not productive of grace but is a reflection of the grace already present in the soul through faith," or words to that effect. Such an answer is, of course, tantamount to rejecting the doctrine of the Real Presence, for to receive the real Christ is to receive His real grace, not a mere reflection of His grace.

Now it was up to the Catholic Church to show me the glorious fulfillment of Christ's promise. And show me she did. Yes, it was in the Catholic Church, the "Roman" Catholic Church, that I found the manna which has come down from Heaven, the Communion bread and wine that are truly the Body and Blood of Christ my Saviour. The Catholic Church declared that it was so, and when I witnessed the profound solemnity of the Consecration on her altar, when I witnessed the radiance and peace that shone on the faces of the communicants, *when I myself felt His Divine Presence pervading the atmosphere,* I had to agree that it must indeed be so.

How could it be otherwise? Could those Catholics and the hundreds of millions that preceded them back through the centuries to the very dawn of Christianity ALL be the victims of hallucination? Hardly. Mass hallucination becomes less prevalent with the advance of civilization, not more prevalent. Hallucinations do not inspire the building of the world's greatest private network of universities and scientific laboratories. Hallucinations do not attract and hold such people as Augustine, da Vinci, Michelangelo, Galileo, Copernicus, Aquinas, Dante, Petrarch, Pasteur and Marconi, people to whom finding the truth is a veritable mania, a sort of religion in itself.

No, this was no hallucination I was witnessing. *Pure and simple, it was faith in the power and integrity of Jesus Christ.* Those Catholics had come to a most realistic conclusion: Jesus Christ is God; therefore He has the power to change bread and wine into His Flesh and Blood on the altar without effecting a change in the appearance of the transformed bread and wine; and Jesus Christ promised that He would do just that for the spiritual nourishment of His faithful; therefore it must be confessed that He is keeping His promise.

In other words, those Catholics were simply believing in the Bible as I was committed in conscience to believe in the Bible. *They were simply believing what Christ expects all of His faithful followers to believe.*

The sacrament of the Real Presence is also called the *Blessed* Sacrament in the Catholic Church—but to me it was a blessed sacrament in more ways than one. For it was my discovery of the true and living Christ in this sacrament of the Catholic Church that inspired me to inquire into her six other sacraments. Did the other six also enjoy an abundance of scriptural support? I wanted to know. Not that I expected to find them without scriptural support. I was quite convinced that the church wherein dwelt the Real Presence of Christ would be the church wherein dwelt the full complement of His sacraments—but I considered it expedient that I should make a complete survey of the Catholic sacraments while I was on the subject, so that my conviction would be confirmed.

Needless to say, my conviction *was* confirmed. One by one I went over the other six with a Catholic priest, and one by one they turned out to be thoroughly grounded in Scripture. No doubt about it, each and every one of them was instituted by Christ, and no doubt about it, each and every one of them imparts grace to the soul, exactly as the Catholic Church teaches.

The following Bible passages established the divine origin, and the great importance, of the Sacrament of Baptism:

"Jesus answered: Amen, amen I say to thee, unless a man be born again of water and the Holy Ghost, he cannot enter into the kingdom of God." (John 3:5). *"Do penance, and be baptized every one of you in the name of Jesus Christ, for the remission of your*

46

sins. . . ." (Acts 2:38). *"And Jesus coming, spoke to them, saying: All power is given to me in heaven and in earth. Going therefore, teach ye all nations; baptizing them in the name of the Father, and of the Son, and of the Holy Ghost."* (Matt. 28:18-19). *"And he said to them: Go ye into the whole world, and preach the gospel to every creature. He that believeth and is baptized, shall be saved: but he that believeth not shall be condemned."* (Mark 16:15-16).

The following Bible passages established that priests have the God-given power to forgive sins in the Sacrament of Penance:

". . . where the disciples were gathered together . . . Jesus came and stood in the midst, and said to them: Peace be to you. . . . As the Father hath sent me, I also send you. . . . Receive ye the Holy Ghost. Whose sins you shall forgive, they are forgiven them; and whose sins you shall retain, they are retained." (John 20:19-23). *"Amen I say to you, whatsoever you shall bind upon earth, shall be bound also in heaven; and whatsoever you shall loose upon earth, shall be loosed also in heaven."* (Matt. 18:18).

The following Bible passages established that the Holy Spirit descends on the newly baptized

47

when the Bishop lays hands on them in the Sacrament of Confirmation:

"Having heard these things, they were baptized in the name of the Lord Jesus. And when Paul had imposed his hands on them, the Holy Ghost came upon them. . . ." (Acts 19:5-6). *"Now when the apostles, who were in Jerusalem, had heard that Samaria had received the word of God, they sent unto them Peter and John. Who, when they were come, prayed for them, that they might receive the Holy Ghost. For he was not as yet come upon any of them; but they were only baptized in the name of the Lord Jesus. Then they laid their hands upon them, and they received the Holy Ghost."* (Acts 8:14-17).

The following Bible passages established that in the Sacrament of Holy Orders God ordains priests to offer up sacrifice for sins, to forgive sins, and to govern His Church:

"Take heed to yourselves, and to the whole flock, wherein the Holy Ghost hath placed you bishops, to rule the church of God. . . ." (Acts 20:28). *"For every high priest taken from among men, is ordained for men in the things that appertain to God, that he may offer up gifts and sacrifices for sins. . . . Neither doth any man take the honor to him-*

48

self, but he that is called by God, as Aaron was." (Heb. 5:1-4). *"And taking bread, he gave thanks, and broke; and gave to them, saying: This is my body, which is given for you. Do this for a commemoration of me."* (Luke 22:19). *". . . the disciples were gathered together . . . Jesus came and stood in the midst, and said to them: Peace be to you. . . . As the Father hath sent me, I also send you. . . . Receive ye the Holy Ghost. Whose sins you shall forgive, they are forgiven them; and whose sins you shall retain, they are retained."* (John 20:19-23). *"And when they had ordained to them priests in every church, and had prayed with fasting, they commended them to the Lord, in whom they believed."* (Acts 14:22). *"For this cause I [Paul] left thee [Titus] in Crete, that thou shouldest set in order the things that are wanting, and shouldest ordain priests in every city, as I also appointed thee. . . ."* (Titus 1:5). *"For which cause I [Paul] admonish thee [Timothy], that thou stir up the grace of God which is in thee, by the imposition of my hands."* (2 Tim. 1:6). *"Neglect not the grace that is in thee, which was given thee by prophecy, with imposition of the hands of the priesthood."* (1 Tim. 4:14).

The following Bible passages established that husband and wife are united, *permanently* united, by God in the Sacrament of Matrimony:

"For this cause a man shall leave his father and mother; and shall cleave to his wife. And they two shall be in one flesh. Therefore now they are not two, but one flesh. What therefore God hath joined together, let not man put asunder. . . . Whosoever shall put away his wife and marry another, committeth adultery against her. And if the wife shall put away her husband, and be married to another, she committeth adultery." (Mark 10:7-12). *"Let women be subject to their husbands, as to the Lord: Because the husband is the head of the wife, as Christ is the head of the church. He is the saviour of his body. Therefore as the church is subject to Christ, so also let the wives be to their husbands in all things. Husbands, love your wives, as Christ also loved the church, and delivered himself up for it. . . . So also ought men to love their wives as their own bodies. He that loveth his wife, loveth himself. For no man ever hated his own flesh; but nourisheth and cherisheth it, as also Christ doth the church: Because we are members of his body, of his flesh, and of his bones. For this cause shall a man leave his father and mother, and shall cleave to his wife, and they shall be two in one flesh. This is a great sacrament; but I speak in Christ and in the church."* (Eph. 5:22-32).

Thus, just as Christ and His Church are inseparably united, so are a man and woman inseparably united in the Sacrament of Matrimony.

The following Bible passages established that the sick and dying receive physical and spiritual balm when they are anointed in the Sacrament of Extreme Unction:

> *"And going forth they preached that men should do penance: and they cast out many devils, and anointed with oil many that were sick, and healed them."* (Mark 6:12-13). *"Is any man sick among you? Let him bring in the priests of the church, and let them pray over him, anointing him with oil in the name of the Lord. And the prayer of faith shall save the sick man: and the Lord shall raise him up: and if he be in sins, they shall be forgiven him."* (James 5:14-15).

And those were not the only Bible passages shown to me. My priest consultant brought my attention to many others. He made it so glaringly obvious that the seven Sacraments of the Catholic Church are Christ's true Sacraments that I found myself blushing with embarrassment, confessing that I must have been in some kind of trance when those passages were in front of me before.

Yes, it was embarrassing to think that the full

import of those Bible passages had escaped me over the years, although I must have read them hundreds of times. But what a joy it was to know that their full import had not continued to escape me. God had indeed answered my prayers for enlightenment.

There was no alternative left now but to become a Catholic and to become one as soon as possible. Every mental reservation I had ever entertained about the great Mother Church of Christendom was now gone, thanks to three great Bible revelations. The Catholic Church, I was firmly convinced, is everything she claims to be; either she is the one true Church of Jesus Christ, His Mystical Body, His infallible teaching voice, His Eucharistic abode, or the Bible is nothing more than a book of fables and the writings of the primitive Christian Fathers nothing more than a collection of pipedreams.

Once my mind was made up it did not take me long to make the transition from Protestantism to Catholicism. And what a glorious adventure it was, too, to become a Catholic, to receive those several weeks of instruction in true Apostolic theology, to make that solemn profession of faith, to receive a Catholic Baptism, to cleanse my soul in the Sacrament of Penance, and then, finally, to receive the living and true Christ in Holy Communion. Believe me, dear reader, there is no adventure more glorious, more satisfying to the soul, this side of Heaven.

The transition was really much easier than I thought it would be. I had imagined that there would be a great storm of resentment within my family and that I would lose a great many very dear friends. I was quite certain that not a single one of my former ministerial colleagues would ever again speak to me, except perhaps to castigate me for being a "traitor." But, surprisingly, that was not the case at all.

After that initial shock, which an announcement of this kind invariably produces, I was confronted not with a wave of bitter resentment, but with a wave of curiosity and wonderment. There were a few instances of ridicule—a few of my acquaintances were more protest-ant than Protestant, more anti-Catholic than pro-Christian—but by and large the freedom of my conscience was respected. By and large the reaction was not "Curse you for doing it!" but "WHY did you do it?" My family and my really close friends knew that I would never defect from Christ—they knew that my loyalty to God and His revealed truth superseded all other loyalties. They simply could not understand why my loyalty to God and His revealed truth had become so suddenly and drastically altered in the mode of its expression.

That took a great deal of explaining, a great deal of very difficult explaining, for it is not easy to translate into words all the things that motivate the soul. But I managed somehow—and with singular success. I say with singular success because shortly afterward my entire family and several of my close friends followed me into the Catholic Church. Yes, once they had the facts, they, too, confessed that the Catholic faith is the true Bible faith—*they, too, wanted the ineffable joy of being united to Christ in the fullness of His Gospel, in the fullness of His Sacraments and in the fullness of His grace.*

How tremendously gratifying that was, to realize that God had not only chosen me to be an object of His grace, but an *instrument* of His grace as well. My gift of faith was indeed a blessed gift of faith, for I could say with another convert named Paul: "Paul, a servant of Jesus Christ, called to be an apostle, separated unto the gospel of God." (*Rom.* 1:1).

Verily, I could sum up my whole confession with that one sentence taken from the Bible.

If I should write a thousand confessions before I die I would be able to sum them all up with that one sentence taken from the Bible. For henceforth my life's principal dedication will be serving Christ. I will not be wearing clerical cloth and I will have no pulpit, but that will not constrain me. I will have His truth and His grace, and I will have my thankfulness for His truth and His grace, which is all I need to outfit me as one of His apostles.

Offering myself as a lay apostle of Christ's holy Church is the least I can do for Him after He has done so much for me.

So call me anything you want to. Call me a religious enigma, call me a slave of papal totalitarianism—call me anything. But while you are calling me these things please keep this in mind: I would not have it any other way. Before I would relinquish one little particle of my Catholic faith I would gladly face the scorn and derision of the entire world. For now, at last, I know real peace of soul, real oneness with Christ my Saviour.

No, I would not have it any other way, and if you, dear reader, should ever become a Catholic, I am sure that you would not have it any other way either.

Sincerely yours in Jesus Christ,

PAUL WHITCOMB